# Journal o
# Chaplain and a
# Family's View of the
# Military and Ways
# to Cope

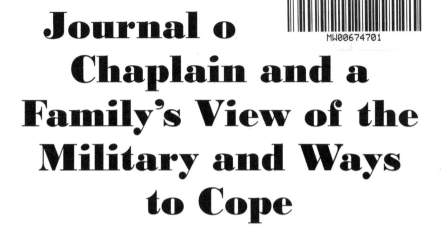

## Dave and Gwyn Page

ISBN 978-1-0980-0951-9 (paperback)
ISBN 978-1-0980-0952-6 (digital)

Christian Faith Publishing, Inc.
832 Park Avenue
Meadville, PA 16335
www.christianfaithpublishing.com

Printed in the United States of America

# Dedication

We salute all military chaplains of all branches of service.
May the Lord bless and protect you and your families back home.

# Preface

The following sermon was delivered at a preaching class at Southern Seminary by my husband, David G. Page. He graduated from seminary in 1963 and continued to serve as pastor at Arcade Baptist Church, in Louisville, Kentucky.

During college and seminary, he held part-time pastorates in Missouri, Indiana, and Kentucky. As you read this sermon, notice that there was no other person teaching or leading Dave during his experience meeting the Lord, Just he himself! The following is an account of that experience.

G. Page

# *Prologue*

Thank you for purchasing this book, and we hope it will help you to find meaning in your walk with the Lord. May the good Lord bless you. If you need to contact us, please call: (252) 288-6868.

Our new address at the local retirement home is:

Dave and Gwyn Page
721 Amhurst Blvd. Apt., .4-B
New Bern, NC 28562

Out of the boiling surf staggered a figure on legs of rubber and collapsed on the sandy beach. Death had been robbed, for this young man had all but perished in the rolling, pounding surf, as the Pacific lashed out with its great power against this secluded Hawaiian beach.

Half a dozen shipmates of the young sailor had watched in terror as he struggled to regain the shore against the strong undertow. They had understood too late why the sign nearby read, *Off Limits To All Military Personnel No Swimming*. And so they watched, miles from help, afraid to help lest they, too, be caught by the undertow. They could see him tire; his head began to roll from side to side and the waves buried him from sight, but he appeared again still struggling. And then when it seemed that there was no hope of his making shore, his feet touched bottom, and with last drop of energy, stumbled to the beach.

After a few minutes of rest, he was strong enough to return to the rented car and continue on the tour of the island with the others. Physically, he was alright, but his mind was in a turmoil. What if he had not made it back to shore? Was he prepared to die? He could recall enough of his Sunday school teaching, though it had been several years now, to know that he was not ready.

His life was in no way related to Jesus Christ. In fact, he held back from committing himself to Christ on several occasions when the invitation had been given in church when he was a lad.

This young man's life was centered around himself. First, he had run away from home at the age of thirteen, and a year later he left high school after completing only one year. For the next few years he had drifted from place to place, until at the age of eighteen, he entered the navy. Three years of this life had made him a hardened sinner whose antics would make the hearts of most saints faint. His paycheck was invariably spent on liquor or lost in a poker game. His vocabulary consisted of four-letter words that only a sailor could fully understand or tolerate for a very long at a time.

But now he had nothing to say. The others laughed talked and whistled at every female that came into view as they drove along, but he was silent. He was thinking, and a voice within him seemed to keep reminding him how foolish he had been to try and live his life without God.

When the day was over the group went to a movie, and then returned to their ship after the lights were out. The other men were soon in their bunks fast asleep, but the young man did not go to bed yet; he was still thinking. He knew what he should do. He should commit his life to God—tonight. A voice within kept telling him that he should, and another kept telling him that he should not. As he walked from the shower room toward his sleeping compartment, he reached his decision. In a voice only God could hear, he called out for help. After he confessed his sins and asked God to forgive him, a sudden feeling of joy and a smile broke across his face for the first time since that morning.

I climbed into my bunk and talked with God for the first time in my life that night. I thanked Him for sparing my life that I might have another opportunity to ask Him to redeem my life, as I felt He had just done. I promised Him that I would serve Him in any way that He should ask.

These events seem a million miles back down the road of life, but I have often looked back at this day, for without reflecting on it, I doubt if I could have weathered the storms which have come since. When problems have arisen and I was frustrated and near despair, I have looked back and remembered that since my life has been related to the eternal God. Though sometimes I am disgusted and ashamed of myself many times, I can remember that since that day my life has been different.

Everyone who attempts to preach must have realization of an encounter with the living God; I am convinced. We must be aware that we do not speak on our own behalf but that we speak on behalf of Him whom we experienced. We cannot tell others what God can do for them apart from our experiences of what He has done for us.

We must have somewhat the same testimony that Amos had when he was forbidden to prophesy at Bethel by the high priest. He said in reply, "I was no prophet, neither was I a prophet's son; but I was a herdsman, and a gatherer of sycamore fruit: and the Lord took me as I followed the flock, and the Lord said unto me, 'Go phophesy unto my people Isreal. Now therefore hear thou the word of the Lord'" (Amos 7:14–16, KJV).

Two times in the book of Acts, Paul makes a reference to his initial encounter with Christ on the Damascus Road. Each time, he points out his former way of life and the change which God has brought to his life since that time. He intends each time to point up that he is not speaking on his own behalf but on behalf of God.

The life of a preacher is difficult, especially for the student minister. When you begin to have nightmares in Greek and Hebrew and a term paper is due in every class at the same time, the deacons at your church become more contrary than usual, the kids get sick, and the wife complains that you are never at home, your finances are low, and, spiritually, the temptation to say "I quit!" often comes. And if you cannot look back on your own life and say "Back there I was lost, undone, and without hope, but now I live in Christ Whom I have come to know by a personal encounter with Him," you will quit.

What I want to share with you today and what I feel must be the testimony of each of us is summed up in these words:

"For I delivered to you as of first importance what I also received, that Christ died for our sins in accordance with the scriptures, that he appeared to Cephas, then to the twelve. Then he appeared to more than five hundred brethren at one time Then he appeared to James, then to all the apostles. Last of all, he appeared also to me" (1 Cor. 15: 3–8, RSV).

Tuesday, 28 Nov. 1967
At sea—Mediterranean

This diary is begun with a note of regret for not having started earlier. This is past the middle of the present deployment which began on 18 Aug. 1967 and is scheduled to end on 31 Jan 1968. This division of destroyers (DES DIV 62) was also deployed in the MED from 15 Feb 1966 to 10 Jul 1966 while I have been assigned as division chaplain.

The purpose of this journal is that it may serve as a record of my feelings, hopes, experiences, etc. to be read in the future for inspiration and instruction to myself, my family, and other interested persons.

This was the 192nd birthday of the Navy Chaplain Corps. The Adams (DDG-2) had a birthday cake, and the captain said some appreciative things about Chaplain Corps earlier last week.

Wednesday, 30 Nov. 1967

At 6:30 this morning, we anchored in Taranto Bay, Italy, for a 6th Fleet Commanders Conference. The religious conference was from 1300 to 1500 onboard the FD *Roosevelt* (*CVA-42*). Chaplain COMSIXthLEEET on Little Rock (CLG-4) was chairman of the conference of about twenty-five chaplains and lay leaders.

The conference could not have been expected to accomplish very much, but I felt that we really used our time in an unworthy manner. The one thing that was worthy, I felt, was that the RADM, COMCARDIV 6, came in and said a few words and then cut the cake, celebrating the 192nd birthday of the Navy Chaplain Corps.

At 1700, we got underway from Taranto Bay. The weather outside is cold and rainy, and the seas seem to be coming up so we may be in for some rough weather.

Thursday, 30 Nov. 1967

The last day of November is a milestone in our time of deployment. There are approximately days to go until we arrive back in the US. Nothing out of the ordinary happened today, but everyone seems to be kept busy. Our schedule today included a gunnery exercise and a night refueling. My time is routinely spent roving around the spaces, talking with the men at work, counseling, reading, studying, and in the evening, playing chess or watching a movie. The hardest things about the life of chaplain on a destroyer is the feeling of being alone, boredom, and separation from one's family. Many of the enlisted men and officers, too, to some degree, do not have time to spend in talking with the chaplain. They are working, on watch, or so tired they must sleep. The one opportunity of the day to draw all of us together is at the time of the evening prayer.

Sunday, 3 Dec. 1967

This was a working day, even though it was Sunday. We had a demonstration for some Belgian VIPs of our ability to highline. Also, there was a missile demonstration. Added to this was a refueling and a rearming. Our Protestant service was held at 1300 between the evaluations (we thought). But the rearming and the refueling details were called away in the middle of the service. Our attendance was fourteen men. There was a mail call this morning, which was the bright spot of the day! I received three letters from home.

Monday–Friday,
4–8 Dec. 1967

On Monday at 09:30, the CF *Adams* anchored at La Ciotat, France. This is a small town of about 20,000 inhabitants. The people seem quite friendly, in general, although the communists are quite active, also. This is the first warship to call here since WWII.

This is a tourist attraction in summer, but now the town is quiet. Hardly any of the people speak English.

Our mail was delayed for three or four days in getting to us. This always hurts morale. There is always some bad news coming in the letters, but most of us are dejected when the mail fails to come for several days running.

The weather here has been windy and cold. This makes for unpleasant conditions for going on liberty because of the boat ride over rough water to the fleet landing.

I've just received word this last week that I will be relieved in March. I am quite ready to be relieved. There are some things about being a destroyer chaplain that I like, but the most difficult thing for me, as is the case with many other men, is the separation from the family. After a while, you just grow numb to the memory of your wife and children. It is hard to explain the feeling. The loneliness is not such a sharp pain anymore. The family seems to sort of slip out of reality; they are part of another world. Time erodes the memory of them, except for occasional vivid flashes brought by letters, pictures, thoughts, etc.

Sunday, 10 Dec. 1967

Our church attendance was only ten this morning. It is hard to say exactly what causes low attendance. On a day like today, I am sure that some of the regular attenders were still asleep.

Monday, 11 Dec. 1967

Today we got underway from La Ciotat, France, at 0930. The day was pretty much routine. We got mail in the p.m. from the carrier. I received three letters and a Christmas package from home.

Tuesday 12 Dec. 1967

Since about 0400 this morning we have had severe weather. Three men were injured from falls during rolls. Some of our rolls have exceeded 40 degrees. The wind has been in gusts of up to 50 mph. Sleeping is a very difficult task because you cannot stay in bed without holding onto something. It is also rough to do any work. The best place to get is in a chair in the wardroom with your back to the bulkhead and bracing your feet against a table or something.

Wednesday, 13 Dec. 1967

The seas are some calmer today. This morning while we were making our approach on the carrier to refuel, a huge wave came over our bow and injured five men seriously. Three of them were later transferred to the carrier (FDR) for medical treatment. We picked up observers from the Tattnall (DDG-2) who will conduct operational readiness inspection (ORI).

Thursday 21 Dec. 1967

Again, we anchored in Aranci Bay, Sardinia, at 0930. I visited the carrier (FDR) Chaplain and did some Christmas shopping.

I found out today that my visit to the FDR on 3 December to conduct services was cancelled. I was supposed to have a communion service and church, while the chaplain was away from the ship. He was on the beach in France making arrangements for their visit later. The reason for the cancellation was because I have been letting my beard grow.

The Admiral doesn't like beards but they are within regulations, so he hates to forbid them (other than on the carrier). He knew I was growing one because I've seen him twice since I've started it on my birthday—October 15.

If I had known that he felt this strongly, I would have shaved rather than have the service cancelled. He had a lay leader lead the service. I don't know if he served communion, but if he did, it is against regulations. Only ordained clergy can do that.

The ironic thing about the whole situation is that the Admiral is a staunch supporter of the religious program and is a Southern Baptist, just like me!

Friday, 22 Dec. 1967

Dear Gwyn,

This is our tenth anniversary; our first of being separated. I could not ask for any more from you during these ten years than you have given. They have been good years. We have had some hard times, but there has never been a time when we were not devoted to each other and have worked together. You share in any success we have made. You have done things that you have not particularly liked without grumbling. I know that you have always had doubts about the Navy chaplaincy, but you have done your very best. I think you have done a magnificent job in all respects, but especially in taking care of the family while I've gone to sea. I only hope and pray that my ministry has been faithful enough to warrant the sacrifices you and the children have made. I love you and am convinced there is not another whom I could love as I love you.

Saturday, 23 Dec. 1967

We anchored at Cannes, France, this morning about 0930 and will stay here until 3 January 1968. This evening, just before the movie on the mess deck, we sang Christmas carols. The turnout was very good, and the participation was enthusiastic. When we arrived today, I took a boat to the carrier (FDR) to visit the chaplain. He had asked me to come out when we got in here but, apparently, he didn't remember that he had, for he seemed surprised to see me.

Sunday, 24 Dec. 1967

The weather was too rough for me to leave the ship to go to the Tattnall for services as I had planned, therefore I only had church on the Adams. The turnout was not much larger than normal, but the carol singing in the evening was well attended. I had my sermon typed and run off for distribution to the crew, since I had written it out in full this week.

Monday, 25 Dec. 1967

Christmas seemed unreal to many of us because we were not in our familiar surroundings and because we are separated from our families. Gwyn, Becky, Carey, and Laura, I want you to know that I am here today instead of with you because I believe God needs someone here to remind those who are in the Navy of his glorious gift of Christ. I'm convinced that God has chosen me for this task, as poor as I am in fulfilling it. Humanly speaking, I would rather be there watching you open your gifts than any place else in the world. With God's help, I'll try to make up to all of you for my absence. You see, I'm here as a volunteer and for what I feel are the highest possible motives, but you, too, are paying a price for this ministry, especially you children are doing so without choice. You may be unaware of the sacrifice you're making now, but someday you will see what you are being asked to give. When you do, don't blame God. If you must feel resentment, blame me. What I hope is that each of you will determine in your own lives to serve God to the best of your ability, even when you have mixed emotions about responsibilities.

Tuesday–Saturday,
26–30 Dec. 1967

These days have been routine. Everyone seems ready to get underway again now that Christmas has passed. Our next big event will be our arrival back in Charleston, S.C. We have approximately thirty days remaining in the cruise. I have been awaiting orders to my next duty station, but they have not arrived yet. I have been informed that my relief will be here on the sixth or seventh of March.

Sunday, 31 Dec. 1967

Today I went by boat across the bay and had 0900 service on the Tattnall. Then I returned to the CF Adams for 1100 service. We had attendances of eleven and thirteen, respectively. Many of the men went ashore to welcome in the new year, but I did not.

Monday, 1 Jan. 1968

There were many this morning who were sleeping off the results of the night before. There were several minor incidents with people who had too much to drink. There were four men late returning from liberty. Most of them were petty officers.

Tuesday, 2 Jan. 1968

There was an all-officer meeting in the wardroom for briefing concerning the operations during the next at sea period. The captain made some comments to the officers after the operations briefing. He is concerned about *behavior ashore*. He seemed to blame the shore patrolmen, officers, and senior petty officers ashore on liberty for not taking charge of potentially explosive situations and exercising their duty and responsibility. Although he made reference to a message from COMSIXTHFLT Admiral on the subject, he failed to mention that COMSIXTHFLT Admiral points out that practically every instance of trouble is trouble that comes *out of a bottle*. He emphasizes that staying sober is the only solution to *conduct ashore*. Maybe the captain does not agree with this, but I'm thoroughly convinced that the admiral is 100 percent correct.

We have been in an exercise that requires our crew to stand condition III watches. This means that after a few days the entire crew gets very tired. This was evident in our church attendance today. We had only four men and myself present. The seas have been quite rough for several days, so most of the men are asleep when not on watch.

Monday, 8 Jan. 1968

Today was another day of rough weather. I do not get seasick, but I get tired of the continual pitching and rolling. Though you put much more of the normal amount of time in bed, you never seem to get rested. It is very noticeable to me that the entire crew is fatigued and irritable from the rough weather and prolonged watch-standing. This exercise will be completed after tonight, and I'm sure that everyone involved is ready for it to be finished. It is only three more weeks until we will be home. Most of the crew are beginning to anticipate our arrival. For me, it cannot come a day too soon.

9–13 Jan. 1968

On Tuesday the ninth, we left the task force and began proceeding toward the Strait of Gibraltar. On Wednesday, we anchored briefly and cleaned sides. Thursday night, we passed through the Strait on arrival at Rota, Spain, at 0930 on Friday, 12 January. That afternoon we had a personnel inspection which was followed by a messing and berthing inspection. Everyone in the crew gripes a lot about the captain having so many inspections. I'm inclined to believe that he is the only one who thinks so many are necessary. He enjoys them for some strange reason. He literally struts around, since he is rather short of stature; he may need these times to fight down an inferiority complex.

He is a good CO, but even good men's faults become apparent when you live so close over an extended period of time. He never seems to let up; if anything, he presses harder every day. Most of the crew dislike him because of his rigid standards in everything, especially military bearing and material condition and cleanliness of the ship.

On Saturday, we left Rota at 1800 to proceed to Marin, Spain, for a four-day visit.

Sunday, 14 Jan. 1968

Today, we are on our way to Marin, Spain, from Rota. Church attendance this morning was thirteen. In the afternoon, the captain assembled the crew to tell them about one of our crew deserting the ship and the Navy while we were in Cannes, France, in December. The man wrote to some of the men in his division and told them he had asked the Soviet Embassy for political asylum. He had left the ship on authorized leave to visit Paris. Apparently, he had planned to defect before he left the ship.

It is obvious that the incident *shook* the entire crew, especially the captain. He probably feels that it will reflect on his ability to command. There will be a thorough investigation, no doubt. The man had asked for transfers off the ship and at least twice to go to Vietnam—both were denied.

Monday,14 Jan., Saturday, 20 Jan. 1968

At 0930 on Monday, we arrived at Marin, Spain. This is the location of the Spanish National Naval Academy. Our task during these days is to show the Spanish midshipmen something of a modem US warship.

On Tuesday, the liaison officer from the American embassy in Madrid took the captain and three other officers, including me, for a tour of the countryside to the town of Santiago de Compostela. This town is a Roman Catholic shrine. It is associated with the burial place of St. James the apostle. On years in which 25 July falls on a Sunday, pilgrimages are made here.

On Wednesday, one of the officers and I went to Vigo, the largest town in the area, and did some shopping. Prices are moderate. This part of Spain is quite pretty and green, even in this time of the year. The hills and the inlets that run back into the valleys from the sea are very beautiful. It is a fishing paradise, I'm told. The people are quite friendly, but mostly poor with primitive farming methods.

On Friday, we departed Marin and arrived in Rota on Saturday morning. We turned over with the CH *Roan* and departed for CONUS at 1500. While in Rota, I received mail from home and news that my new duty station will be 2nd Marine Division, Camp Lejeune, North Carolina.

I'm not overjoyed at the new duty station but will try not to form any opinions against going there. I'm praying that God will lead us to serve him there. I'm happy now that at least we will soon be together again as a family.

Sunday, 21 Jan. 1968

Today was a quiet day of steaming. Our church attendance was fifteen. I served communion today.

Monday, 22 Jan. 1968

At 1300 today, we arrived in Ponta Delgada, Azores, for refueling and departed at 1700. The day was another quiet day of steaming. We are inside the last week of our deployment. The time cannot pass too quickly for any of us. The weather so far has been fine for which I am truly thankful.

Tuesday–Friday, 23–26 Jan. 1968

We have been storming steadily toward home. The weather has been most cooperative. Only for brief periods have the swells been large enough to be noticeable or to make it uncomfortable aboard.

On Wednesday we learned of the North Korean attack and capture of an American naval vessel, the *US Pueblo*, an AEGI, off their coast. Our news has been scanty, but we have learned that the president is trying to settle the problem by diplomatic means. At the same time, a task force has been sent to the area and about 14,000 air and naval air reservists have been called to active duty.

The captain is quite adamant in saying that the CO of the Pueblo did not do his duty as a naval officer in letting his ship be captured and without resistance. (Their messages emphasized that they offered no resistance to the patrol boats that came alongside and boarded her.)

Most officers feel that we should take immediate military action to recover the ship and her crew of eighty. I fear the military action may be necessary, but I'm happy that a great message emphasized that they offered no resistance to the patrol boats that came alongside and boarded her.

I'm happy that a great nation such as ours can exercise restraint in the use of her superior force. I do feel that somehow the Navy failed in letting the ship fall into the hands of the North Korean communists' hands. I pray that the situation can be settled without any more military action.

Thursday, 4 April 1968

Many days have passed that seem to have kept me from keeping this journal up during this long period. We arrived in the US on 29 January. There are no words to express the joy of returning to home and family. In mid-February, Gwyn and I drove to Camp Lejeune for a two-day visit of the area and to meet the division chaplain. We learned that I will be deploying again in July. This didn't make us too happy since I'd just finished three years of sea duty and would have to go to sea again in a few months.

On 8 March, I detached from DesDiv 62. We visited my brother, Tom Page, ATC, USN in Jacksonville, Florida, for a couple of days, and then proceeded to the Camp Lejeune area. We stayed four nights in a trailer on Onslow Beach while looking for a place to live. House-hunting was difficult and discouraging. Everything that we were interested in buying or renting had a long waiting period before we could move in. Finally, we decided to rent a house on Queen's Creek Rd. It is five miles from Swansboro and three and a half miles from the Triangle Outpost Gate (back gate) to the base. This was the only house for rent that we saw; there were just none available at all! The house was pretty dirty and the yard was trashy, but Gwyn has done a marvelous job on the place. We have room for a garden (which we got planted last Saturday).

In Charleston, we bought a dog and named it Snoopy. He's one-half Gordon Setter (father) and one-half Irish Setter (mother). He was three months old when we got him. He has become a part of the family. He seems intelligent and has a natural talent for retrieving. Monday, 18 March, I checked into the 2nd Marine Division. After some indoctrination at Field Medical School and Counter Guerrilla Warfare School, I was assigned to 3rd Battalion, 2nd Marines on March 21. The chaplain, whom I relieved, stayed with me for approximately one week, helping me get familiarized.

The commanding officer of 3rd Battalion, 2nd Marines is a Southern Baptist. He seems to be a fine Christian man who is intensely interested in the moral and spiritual welfare of his men.

30 July 1968

It seems that this journal is neglected more than it is kept up. The period since joining 3rd Battalion, 2nd Marines has been a busy one. After a few weeks, I was assigned with another chaplain at the worship service at Midway Park.

In early June, we took a camping trip home. We only had fourteen days, but I think they were a good two weeks together. We did see my mother and Gwyn's parents, as well as most of the rest of the family. On Sunday, the sixteenth of June, we came back by Arcade Baptist Church in Louisville, Kentucky, and I spoke at the morning worship service. We had a good time seeing old friends again. At present, I am on the USS *Montrail APA-213* on my way to the Mediterranean again. We left Sunny Point, North Carolina, on Saturday, 27 July, and are to arrive back in Camp Lejeune on about 15 December. Today, we continue to steam at about 16 knots across the Atlantic. The weather is good so there is practically no seasickness, even though the Marines have mostly never been to sea before. There were seven present today for devotions at 1615. The recreation room (B-comp) is not an adequate place for any kind of service, but it is as good as this ship affords.

Saturday, 2 Aug. 1968

We have been steaming steadily eastward as before. Today we got our bulletin for tomorrow's service on board. It helps greatly to have a clerk assigned. My clerk, Chuck, is very conscientious in his work. He has to operate the library so that we may set up our field desk in the space. This evening I received word that in the p.m. tomorrow I will go to the USS *San Marcos* and the PHIBRON. Two chaplains will move over here till we get to our turnover point next week. The moving is inconvenient, but I do desire to get to as many ships and serve as many men as possible. I wrote a letter home tonight. I do miss the family intensely, although we've only been gone a little over a week.

Thursday, 5 Sept. 1968

During the past month we have been kept quite busy. On the ninth of August we had our turnover at Almeria, Spain. My contact was a chaplain from the other BLT. Being Catholic, he didn't have much to give me by way of a program. He did pass on some information on tours. We stopped for two days in Malta on the twelfth and thirteenth of August, then proceeded on to Nea Paramos, Greece, for our first landing. This was my first experience in going ashore with the Marines. It was an enjoyable eight days, if somewhat inconvenient at times.

On Sunday, 25 August, I conducted my first service ashore with Marines. It was held outside on a hillside in the battalion command post. There were thirty men in attendance. Also, the Catholic chaplain came ashore and had mass for the Marines that day.

We are presently visiting Izmir, Turkey. On Tuesday of this week, I went on a tour to Ephesus. This is some strange power that grips you when you realize that you are standing where some of the events recorded in the Bible took place.

Mail has been very slow in both directions. This is a dampening factor on morale when it takes so long to get answers to letters that you write. To the present, letters have been seven or eight days coming to me. This is unsatisfactory. Before, in the Mediterranean, I have received letters in three or four days.

Sunday, 8 September 1968

Saturday morning at 0900 we got underway from Izmir. Today we had no transfer of chaplains to other ships. We had about forty-two in the Protestant service on board. I served communion to about thirty-five of the men. Tonight, we are going to bed early because we have an 0300 reveille for a rehearsal landing at Nafplion, Greece. The Marines and I will actually land on Tuesday morning, about daylight.

Saturday, 7 December 1968

During the past three months, the BLT has been in the Mediterranean. We have made landings in Greece, Turkey, Sardinia, and Spain. We are now on our way home. Our turnover was on 27 November at Carbonaras, Spain. The time of our arrival back in Morehead City, NC, is 0800 on 10 December, so we are getting short.

As I reflect back on the cruise, there have been some complaints that I would make. One, there has been no place provided to me for privacy in counseling. I spoke to the XO of the ship about this early in the cruise, but he was not concerned nor helpful in this matter. On our return trip, I have been leading daily devotional studies. The men seem to enjoy these, and I think they have been the most rewarding thing about the whole cruise.

Gwyn, kids, there are not words to express how I long to be home once more. The separation has been worse this time than the times before, it seems.

I applied for augmentation into the regular Navy and should have been considered by the board which met in October. At the present time, I have not heard the results. I have mixed feelings about staying in the Navy that I cannot take another tour of sea duty after this tour, and I understand that for rotation purposes, this is considered shore duty.

Monday 26 January 1970

Again, this journal has been neglected, but I will briefly review the past thirteen months since the last entry:

In January 1969, I was selected for augmentation into the regular Navy. Any questions I had must now forever be forgotten. In the last part of January, we moved into government quarters at Camp Lejeune (3174 MOQ). In February, we purchased a sixteen-foot travel trailer. I also acquired an Irish Setter pup in January because my other dog died.

In April, I killed my first wild turkey on the base. In June, we took fifteen days and went to Missouri with the new trailer. It was a wonderful trip.

My orders for 1st MAW, FMF (RVN) came in August, and on 16 October, we departed Camp Lejeune. In the next thirty days, we moved to Liberty, Missouri (504 College St.), and spent our last days together as a family that we would have for a long time.

I got to quail hunt for two days with my old friend, Paul Branstetter, in south MO near Licking. Also, we did some duck and goose hunting.

On 16 November (Sunday), I boarded a plane for Camp Pendleton, California. Then on to Vietnam on 24 November, arriving *in country* on 30 November 1969.

After a week in Da Nang, I was assigned to the chapel at Phu Bai, eight miles from Hue. I was there six weeks with a Catholic chaplain. It was a good time.

On 15 January 1970, I reported to MAG-13 in Chu Lai to relieve a chaplain who was due to rotate in February.

Yesterday, Sunday, 25 January 1970, in the middle of our service, about ten hundred (10 AM) the base was attacked by rockets. We had to secure the service. It was my first exposure to fire, if indeed you can call it exposure. There were eight rockets, probably 120 mm, in all that hit the area. There were no injuries at all from the attack.

Today I conducted a memorial service for three men who were recently killed in action. They were all members of the 1st Combined Action Group. I was assisted by a RC/chaplain from the Army.

There were many other attacks on the base, and many more marines and sailors wounded or killed during my tour in Vietnam, but this is the end of my journal—but not the end of my ministry.

\*\*\*\*\*\*\*\*\*\*\*\*\*\*\*\*\*\*\*\*\*\*\*

The following accounts were taken from letters, dialogues, and understanding of the actions taken by Chaplain Page.

By G. Page, Navy wife

While still at Chu Lai, he visited two Catholic orphanages with a nun and saw the need for baby food and warm jackets for the children. When it rained it was quite chilly, so they needed small jackets.

Chaplain Page wrote to the International Orphans, Inc., in Los Angeles, and they sent 600 cases of baby food to the two orphanages.

Dave served in Vietnam from the fall of 1969 to December 1970, counseling, preaching on Sunday in the chapel, or in the jungle with Marines. During the week, he and the Catholic chaplain went by helicopter to the platoons stationed in the mountains or in the bush to have service or be with the men.

Sometimes, if the army chaplain was away, he visited the sick and wounded soldiers and marines at the army hospital.

At the end of his tour in Vietnam, he received orders to the hospital in Pensacola. But this duty required him to attend a three-month clinical training course in Bethesda, MD. This time, the family tagged along!

The tour at the hospital in Pensacola was from 1971 to 1974. His job was intense, since he was the only chaplain. Sometimes he would just get home in the evening and receive a telephone call with an emergency. There was a small chapel alongside the hospital, so Dave preached each Sunday. Our children served as acolytes, lighting candles and taking up the offering.

Dave mentioned that the duty in Vietnam and the hospital were more intensive and effective than any other.

New orders arrived in late summer of 1974 for Pearl Harbor, Hawaii. We were overjoyed! Dave was chaplain of a squadron of eighteen ships—tugs, salvage, and two oilers.

After two years, he received new orders to Camp Lejeune, North Carolina again. He was at 1st Battalion, 2nd Marines for a few months, and later transferred to a regiment at headquarters.

About the end of his tour, he received a phone call and was told he made the rank of Commander. This required him to attend the Senior Course in Newport, Rhode Island. Our family tagged along again, and we enjoyed living in New England. The course was one year, so afterward we moved near the duty station of Norfolk, Virginia.

His orders were to the aircraft carrier, the USS *America*. He was there from 1979 to 1981. There were three chaplains assigned to the carrier—two Protestants and one Catholic. They made many cruises to the Mediterranean, Indian Ocean, and Caribbean. There was much work to be done, especially when the pilots and aircraft were on board—around 6,000 men.

Dave spent three years on the carrier. When they were at sea, he went by helo to the other ships that were in their group, sometimes preaching five or six times on Sunday. The America and her group also crossed the equator and went down the Suez Canal and in the Indian Ocean. Several wives and myself met the ship when it landed in Perth, Australia. It was a long cruise of seven months, and we met halfway through it. The Aussies were very hospitable people. I'd like to go back there again for more than the five days we had.

We are sorry to say that our son's drinking problem grew more intense, even though he attended AA and NA meetings and a temperance program where he was sober for a whole year. But a big problem arose in his life and he went back to drinking. We lost Carey in an auto accident in 1985. He was only twenty-three years old.

In 1981, Dave's orders were in the same area of Norfolk. He was Senior Chaplain of Public Works and Naval Housing units in Norfolk, Virginia. Ben Morell Chapel was in the middle of the housing complex, so Dave preached each Sunday besides all the counseling of the housing. He was there from 1981 to 1983.

The last tour he had was at CRUDESGRUP-8 in Norfolk, too. He was Senior Chaplain of about twelve chaplains on forty ships, being two battleships, cruisers, and destroyers.

Dave says the chaplaincy was good experience and ministry, but the separation from the family for long periods was stressful.

He retired on December 1, 1987 with the ceremony on the cruiser the USS *Virginia*.

So after four years as an enlisted man, two years reserves, and twenty-two and a half years as a Navy chaplain, his military career ended. But that doesn't mean his ministry did!

He pastored a church, Carrow Baptist Church, in Virginia Beach for three years, then we went to the mission field in Morocco for five years, then in Ukraine for three.

We have retired from the mission field, but we're now just *shifting gears*. When the Lord calls you to do full-time service, it doesn't end. Dave preaches when he gets an opportunity, and we both taught English as a second language to refugees and people that need to learn to read.

Dave learned he has non-Hodgkin's lymphoma (caused by Agent Orange in Vietnam.) He took chemo treatments for eight years, every six months. It left him with severe neuropathy in his limbs.

We feel the military was good for our family, even though we moved a lot. That was the least of our problems. Our kids learned that when life threw them a curve, *you keep on keepin' on.* They were not afraid to meet new people and new circumstances with an open mind.

# A Family's View of the Military and Ways to Cope

D ave and his brother, Tom, left home on the farm at a young age to escape a cruel stepfather. There was not much work to be had in southern Missouri, so they headed to Kansas to work in the wheat harvests. From there they headed and worked in Oklahoma. Hitch-hiking back to the farm when there was no work, they returned to high school.

Two brothers and friends joined them as they traveled to Colorado, Oregon and Washington to pick fruit. The way they were living—hand-to-mouth—had no more of a chance to succeed than a snowball in a hot skillet!

Later, Dave and his brother worked in a large corporation in northern Kansas City for a few years. Because they were registered for the draft, they decided to enlist in the Air Force or Navy. They wanted to join the Air Force but didn't want to wear a tie every day, so they joined the Navy in 1952. After boot camp, they were selected to go to aviation electronics school. So they got a job, trained for it, and got to see the rest of the world too.

After completing four years of enlisted service in the Navy, Dave and I met at a young people's meeting in church. Prior to this, in 1955, he nearly drowned in a riptide in Hawaii. He then made a decision to turn from his ways and follow the Lord the same evening. After thoroughly reading the scriptures and through the Lord's lead-ing, he felt called to the ministry.

After completing only one year of high school, he had lots of schooling to finish. He received a GED while still in the Navy and enrolled at a junior college in southern MO, with the advice of our pastor. He was ordained in 1957 and had student pastorates while attending college and seminary.

He was awarded a Fellowship from Duke University but turned it down since he knew the Lord wanted him in the ministry and he needed to go to seminary instead.

Dave introduced himself to me as "A country boy," growing up in the Ozarks of Missouri. We dated in the summer of 1957, and I realized over that time that I had never met or dated a young man who was so devoted to the Lord as he. When I looked into his big brown twinkling eyes, I trusted him and knew I was falling for him. We could talk about anything, and I enjoyed his Irish wit.

By the end of the summer, he kissed me goodnight and it nearly "knocked my sox off!" The next week he proposed, and I confessed to him that, "I did not know how to play the piano" (I guess I thought all preachers' wives had that responsibility). Then he said he didn't care; he only wanted to marry me. And we were married during his Christmas break of that year.

Soon after, we went to school together; he in his last semester of junior college and my first semester. We were like most newlyweds— so poor we couldn't *pay attention.* But the Lord saw to our needs and helped us through college and three of years of seminary.

He served in student pastorates in Missouri, Indiana, and Kentucky for a total of nine years. The last pastorate in Kentucky was a student pastorate while completing his final year of seminary, and it turned into a full-time job for three years.

While pastoring this church, he was in the Navy Reserves and preached early each Sunday at the Reserve Center, then went to our own church for Sunday school and church services. It was during this time (when the Vietnam conflict escalated) that he felt called by the Lord to enter the chaplaincy full-time. So, after much prayer by both of us, he was accepted by the Navy as a full-time chaplain and the Home Mission Board of the SBC. Soon after, he went to Newport, Rhode Island, to Chaplain School.

After three months of school, our family of five (three small children and Dave and I) headed off to his first duty station in Charleston, SC. He was the chaplain of three destroyers, and I learned the military was a different scenario from being the pastor's wife of a local church! After getting us settled in a rental house, Dave deployed for five months on a Mediterranean cruise.

Our children were three, four, and five and a half, and it was a big shock to them, as well as me, not to have Daddy come home for supper. We found one way to cope with loneliness which was to *keep busy and find new interests. We also went to the library. It's free, and there are books for the whole family.*

We all enjoyed reading together. When the children were quite small, we read a book together at naptime. Everyone climbed on our double bed and we read a story after lunch. One by one, they drifted off to sleep, and sometimes I was the first one. Later on, when they were school age, we read after bath time. One of their favorite books was *The Secret Garden.* I wanted the children to know the world that can open before them by reading.

There were many children in Navy housing, and after seeing children the same age as ours, I asked them if they'd like to have a *story time* on a blanket under a tree. Many came, and we read all sorts of books, but mainly small books with a Bible emphasis. These were books Dave received from a someone who gave them to him. We read stories of the Ten Lepers, the Good Samaritan, etc. It was my hope the children would remember them. Most of them did not go to Sunday school or chapel.

*Going to the zoo is a good way to spend your time.* The zoo in Charleston was small but interesting. Our children liked feeding day-old bread to the ducks, geese, and swans, and watching them fight over it! They also liked visiting the one-eyed lion, the bear with three legs, and the foul-mouthed parrot (he was kept behind a double-paned glass so no one could hear his bad language he'd learned from an old ship's captain). The kids liked to watch the monkeys and throw peanuts to them. They all liked the zoo, and it was free, so I did, too.

Battery Park was a good place to go too. Our kids liked to feed the seagulls stale bread and climb on the old canons. I used to like to see the different colored houses on Rainbow Row and wonder what the town looked like a hundred years before. In good weather, *we went to the beach to swim and build sand castles.*

Since our whole life had been built around the church, I made sure the children were in Sunday school and church each Sunday.

But to my amazement, the pastor and his wife of the Baptist church, where we joined, acted like they didn't want us there. So the children and I drove to the Navy base and attended the chapel service. We were with other military families and felt welcome. On other tours, we always joined a local Baptist church so the children could be in Sunday school and children's mission groups. Every other place welcomed us.

I won't forget our first cocktail party (it was a command performance for officers). There were many people crowded into the XO's living and dining rooms, and everyone had a glass in their hand. Of course, I knew there was lots of liquor circulating, but I didn't want to be a part of that. Since my father was an alcoholic, I tried to stay away from it since it caused so much distress in our family. I saw a punch bowl on the dining room table and opted for that because I'd made many bowls of fruit punches with fruit juices and ginger ale and ice added. But after two punch cups of it, I knew something was amiss. I was *really hot,* especially my ears! When I met up with my husband in that crowded place, he said, "Don't drink the punch. It's *not* Baptist punch!" I told him I already had and was feeling the effects of it. We made a hasty retreat, and when we got home, it took me two hours to open two cans of tomato soup and make toasted cheese sandwiches for our family. Let's face it, I was *smashed!*

All through college and seminary days, we had hoped to be appointed as foreign missionaries one day. I felt we were in a foreign land when we moved from the Midwest to Charleston. The local people ate rice every day, it rained most of the time, the children weren't used to the weather and were constantly sick, and I couldn't understand a word the Charlestonians were saying. After a few months, we grew accustomed to the new place, and we liked it a lot. I even began to understand the *gullah* talk. As soon as Dave reentered the Navy, I knew it would be a different life and I was bound and determined to like it. I also realized that I was a part of it since I'd heard the saying, "Those who wait are also part of the Navy."

Every time Dave deployed, I found I died a little whenever he left. A military wife's greatest fear is to see a black car park in her driveway and see two uniformed officers (a chaplain and casualty officer) inform her that her husband was killed.

How did we deal with the deployments? "We just learned to live with it." It was Dave's new job, and the children and I realized life wasn't going to be what it used to be. The Lord had called him to this new job, and with the Lord's help we'd all get through it. Lord Tennyson wrote that, "The parting of a husband and wife is like the cleaving of a heart; one half will flutter here, one there."

I found that *reading library books or magazines and watching movies on TV* were good ways to help me when I felt lonely. Of course, with three little ones to care for, there wasn't much time to feel that way. *writing letters to your loved one makes you feel closer to them,* so Dave and I wrote a letter to one another every day.

I kept a *big picture of Dave* in the living room where the children could see it, and so they would feel connected to him. *We also prayed for him at mealtimes and at bedtime.* The children drew pictures for him that were included in my letters. We also made cassette recordings and sent those. (Remember those days?) All this was before the days of cell phones and the internet. Even though we wrote every day, sometimes we wouldn't get mail for a week, then one day we'd receive three or four letters.

In one letter Dave wrote that he had been to a restaurant in Barcelona, Spain, that served snails and mentioned how good they were. Our four year-old daughter remembered months later and asked her daddy when he returned home from deployment, "Daddy, did you really eat nails?"

When the ship returned from deployments, it was a happy day for all of us. Except for our youngest daughter, Laura, who hid behind the sofa and was too timid to come out and talk to her father.

It took a long time to get reacquainted, and she finally got used to him having a beard and being gone to sea a lot.

We moved into Navy housing (Hunley Park) while Dave was deployed, so for all of us, it was a new home. After the kids went to kindergarten and first grade, I went back to college to finish my degree. At other duty stations, I worked in Navy Relief or Red Cross. Dave's tour in destroyers was extended, so it was a three-year tour with lots of deployments. Holidays were the worst to get through, and we'd usually *meet with other ship wives and their children to share a meal,* with each bringing food. After the meal the kids played together, while we women found out what the men were doing and where the ship was going from the captain's wife.

When Dave was at sea, he wrote about a sailor who was very anxious about his pregnant wife. She needed a friend to talk to, and she had written to her husband that she was going to take her own life if he didn't come home soon! So the kids and I went to visit her and console her with the fact that life will go on, even if she and my husband were at sea. Our children stayed in the front yard until I approached her and found that she had no weapon on her. Then I tried to get her to call other ship wives, especially the ombudsman to help her. It seemed to calm her when she saw our small children, and we were glad we went to visit her.

His next tour of duty was with 2nd Marines, 3rd Battalion at Camp Lejeune, NC. That's right. The Navy provides chaplains, doctors, nurses, lawyers. dentists, dental techs, corpsmen, and medical service corps at Marine bases.

We lived off base in Hubert, and were on a long waiting list for base housing. During that time, I had a terrible toothache and called a dentist nearby to get an appointment. The dentist answered, and when I asked him for an appointment for a filling, he said, "I don't fill 'em, lady. I just pull 'em!" I finally found a dentist in Jacksonville and got a filling. It took eight months, but we finally got in housing in Stone Street. It was one-half block to the elementary school, so the children could walk to school, and we all liked it there.

Even our dog liked it. He was an outside dog and didn't like to be staked to a pin or his leash to the clothesline, so he yelped a lot.

I figured the neighbors didn't like the noise, and I felt sorry for him and let him loose, just until he brought home a fur stole. He'd taken it off someone's clothesline where they probably draped it over it to air out. What to do? I took it to the nearest neighbor and saw that she was gone, so I draped it over her clothesline. Then Snoopy was secured to his tether again!

When Dave returned home, he was counseling a Marine who wanted to go home and get married (as most did). He leaned over and said, "Chaplain, you don't know what it's like to be in love!" The pictures of our three children were sitting on his desk, so he pointed to them and said, "Yes, I do." You see, many in the military think that most chaplains are Catholic.

The fee for cleaning military housing (by private individuals) was $250 to $350 (in the 60s) when a family vacated one. This fee rackled my Scottish nature, *so in order to avoid that expense, I started the cleaning myself as soon as Dave knew orders were coming.* For the final inspection, inspectors came to the housing unit and did a *white glove* inspection, taking the kitchen range apart and running their white gloves around it, the window sills, door frames, inspecting walls, appliances, etc. It's amazing what 409 cleaner can do. It makes a fingerprinted wall look like it's just been painted. We passed all of our inspections, thank goodness!

A veteran Navy wife told me to *use the same curtains and bedspreads in the children's rooms in the new residence and the kids will not be so upset at moving so often.* Then you can change them later on if you like. I used the idea for kitchen curtains, too. This was sage advice and I used it, but it didn't help the school situation any!

After two years, my husband's next tour was with 2nd Marine Air wing in Vietnam. We moved out of housing to our college town of Liberty, Missouri, not far from our families. As the moving truck pulled away, the Navy detailer called. Dave answered, and the detailer asked if we were already moved in.

Dave told him the truck had just pulled away. And the man said, "I was going to cancel your orders, but if you have already moved in, go ahead and go to Vietnam." I began to wonder if that detailer had been drinking some of that punch I'd had!

Now, as grownups, our kids say they feel that the town of Liberty, Missouri, is like their hometown after moving every two or three years. The elementary school was so close they could walk there, except on cold winter days. Wouldn't you know, the winter of '69 was the coldest it had been in fifty years! I took a part-time job of substitute teacher in their elementary school which kept me pretty busy. When not substituting, I worked in the health room as a substitute nurse. Actually, it was using lots of band-aids. Our second grader knew when I worked there, so she routinely got a *stomachache* on the days I was there and wanted to come and lie own on the cot and see Mama.

Dave visited several orphanages while in Nam and wrote that a nun said the children needed coats of all sizes since it got cold there at night in the rainy season. He included that need in one of his letters, so I put a notice in the local paper of that need, and as a result, had a huge supply of used coats that showed up on our doorstep. I mended some, laundered others, and we sent lots of boxes to Dave so he could distribute them to several orphanages. Our Women's Missionary Society at our local Baptist church paid for the SAM postage. Gerber foods also donated a whole helicopter full of baby food after Dave wrote them of the need.

He didn't tell me until after he got home, but one time when he and the Catholic chaplain were dropped at an outpost, a Marine ran up to them and said, "We're glad you got through. The last helo was shot down! Did you bring any mail?" Dave and the Catholic chaplain were usually dropped at different outposts, then the helo would go back and pick up one of them and drop them at the other outpost. Sunday services were held on the base when not under attack.

My, how we enjoyed Dave's R and R in Hawaii for five days, about halfway through his tour in Vietnam. We never dreamed we'd live there some day in that beautiful place.

While my husband was in Vietnam, I had times when I was feeling really *down*. He had been at sea for several years in Charleston, then on shore duty. He went to sea for another five months, followed by thirteen months in Nam. I'd nearly forgotten what he looked like sometimes. But I knew I had to pull myself out of the *pity potty* for the children's sake. It wasn't his fault; he was just following orders. I had to come back to the real world, so I remembered what Phil. 4:13 said, "I can do everything through Him, who gives me strength." Thank heavens for the Lord to always pull us through a hard time. A person can tell Him their troubles at any hour, since He stays up all night!

When Dave returned to finish his tour in Vietnam after our R and R, it felt good for both of us, knowing his tour was about over. But it didn't make it any easier for him. He still went into the bush with a driver in a jeep (with the driver's rifle by his side) or by helo when it was possible to the outposts in the mountains.

When Laura was eight, she had some questions about death and said she was afraid to die. It seems some boys at school told her that her daddy was going to get killed in Vietnam! It was a cruel thing to tell her, but I reassured her that someone was there beside him with a gun and the Lord was watching over him at all times. Then I quoted John 3:16 to her, "For God so loved the world, He gave His only begotten son that whosoever believed in Him should not perish but have everlasting life." Then, taking out the word *whosoever* and putting her name there made a difference.

After telling her that if she asks the Lord to forgive her of her sins (like lying, being mean to someone, or not obeying us), the Lord would forgive her. She must put her faith in Him, and live for Him. We prayed then, and she accepted the Lord as her Savior.

Afterward, our son, Carey, heard us from his bedroom and said he wanted to do the same thing. He was nine, and we followed the same procedure as with Laura.

So both children came to know the Lord on the same evening—what *joy!* Our older daughter, Becky, made a decision to accept the Lord at camp some years earlier. When Dave returned home, our pastor allowed him to baptize the two youngest ones at our church.

After being in the chaplaincy for seven years, my husband had been gone for six of them on deployments, so when he received orders to the hospital in Pensacola, we decided the kids and I would tag along for his three-month clinical training in Bethesda, MD. Our kids were in the best school district they had ever been in there—in

Montgomery County. It was a progressive school, and they enjoyed it. We all enjoyed seeing the sights of DC area as a family, too, on the weekends.

My husband was the only chaplain at the hospital in Pensacola, but he loved the duty there and in Vietnam. He said each of those places were intensive duty (I suppose because of the near-death situations). We bought our first home in Pensacola, and the kids—in fourth, fifth, and sixth grades—say it was their favorite place to live. Dave's tour was extended to three years, and it was a 24/7 day job. He would just get home from the hospital and ready to sit down to supper and the phone would ring with some emergency, so he'd have to go back. Word came from Washington that long-distance moves would be limited, so we hoped the orders would be at Jacksonville, Florida, where his brother was stationed.

A friend from the local Baptist church asked me if I'd like to help her start a *coffee talk* class in a nearby trailer park. I agreed, so we asked the owner of the park for permission and she said we could do that and even offered to let us have it in a large room in the office. Then she said she would babysit the little ones! We sent a flyer around the park advertising the meeting and offering coffee, a Bible study, and craft class afterward. There was a big turnout of young women who were mostly military wives. They were far from home and needed a place to meet and have new interests. Several of them started going to church services.

This is a great way to meet non-Christians. Think of how many trailer parks there are across America!

You can imagine how surprised we were to learn his new orders were for Pearl Harbor, HI! We were jubilant about moving there. Dave was to be chaplain of eighteen ships' chaplains in Service Group Five. We were fortunate to get on the housing list quickly. Private homes were very nice but sky-high prices. We learned a person could buy a house but not the land. It was rented from the government. The Navy housing department offered us a four-bedroom unit which backed up to Pearl Harbor. We were overjoyed that Dave was assigned one there. We could see Eva Beach from our lanai (screened porch). There was a banana, mango tree, and tennis court in our backyard, too.

I was in seventh heaven going to free craft and tennis classes, but our kids had a different story. We had two in middle school and a freshman in high school, and our sponsor never informed us to enroll them in private schools before we arrived in August. (He was a Catholic priest, so he was unaware of the school situation.) So I thought, *What could be wrong with public schools?* But I soon learned that most of the teachers were Japanese with heavy accents, and our kids couldn't understand them. The band director said our kids couldn't get in middle school band because they didn't sign up for it in the spring. The vice principal and I had a *little talk* about it not being fair. Our kids owned their own instruments and had been playing since sixth grade. Most of the other students rented theirs. Our son had been the student director in seventh grade. When I acted like a *mama bear protecting her cubs,* the vice principal finally consented and they got to be in band, but that was the only good news we had.

The majority of the students were Japanese, Sumatran, and Filipino who made life rough for the black and white students. Not many Hawaiian students attended the schools where our children attended. Every day the kids would rush home and head for the bathrooms, since they were afraid to use the ones at school. The rough students would surround them and steal lunch money, jewelry, and watches. Becky came home after the first few days and rushed upstairs to her bedroom and fell across the bed, crying, "Mom, you've *got* to take us back to America!" When I questioned her, she said she and the other *houlies*—Hawaiian for white people—were stoned with prunes in the courtyard, trying to get to their classes. I asked, "Why did they throw prunes?" And she said dried prunes were on the lunch trays and they used those. We kept trying to enroll them in private schools (which were very expensive), but to no avail. There was no place where we could return to the mainland since our families didn't have room for us to move in with them. *If I had it to do over again, I'd homeschool them!*

It was a good thing Dave answered the phone in the middle of the night instead of me! If a person was planning on committing suicide, he could talk him out of it. But if I'd answered in my sleepy state, I probably would have said, "Oh, go ahead and jump!" so I could get back to sleep. One night a woman called about 3:00 a.m. and said, "Chaplain, you've got to do something about all these bugs in our apartment!" He calmly said, "There's not a thing I can do about it now. I'll call the housing department in the morning if you'll give me your name and address, okay?"

Our son Carey had never seen kids drink alcohol or take drugs, but he began to do the same things while he was with them. It was the military dependents who offered them to him. He went from an A and B student to Ds and Fs. We were astounded and took him for counselling by several professionals after our talks with him were to no avail. The last year we were there, there were four students killed at a football game at a high school near our government housing. This was not the school Becky attended.

Dave and Carey took a scuba diving course together, and we bought a catamaran boat that they could take out on the bay. Both of these endeavors were so Dave could spend some time with him so he'd have new interests.

The kids loved going to the beach, and all played ball with the other military kids in the housing development. At other times, the girls were cheerleaders for football games. Carey's favorite activity was *mud sliding* in the misty rain that came every day. The kids used garbage can lids, folded boxes, etc. to slide on. They also loved to go to the Aloha Stadium for concerts of big name stars.

Becky remembers Hawaii with the beautiful, vivid colors of the rainbows she saw at softball practice. Every day when she went from school to practice she saw the rainbow at 4:30 p.m. She remembers Hawaii being the most beautiful place she'd ever been.

Laura and Carey decided to take paper routes in the Navy housing area. They used their bikes to make the routes, then Carey decided to use his skateboard. It was funny to watch him glide around the corners barefooted, throwing papers.

Laura had taken horseback riding lessons at the stable in Pensacola and riding in Hawaii, too. She decided she would take the money she made babysitting and from her paper route and buy a horse when we got back to the mainland. Her father explained that a horse needs someplace to run and a stable which can be expensive. So, undaunted, she decided to spend all her money on a pair of shoe skates!

When we left Hawaii and landed at the LA airport, the kids all said, "Hallelujah, we're back in America!"

Moving was the toughest on the kids when they were teenagers since they had to leave their friends and girl and boyfriends. Becky said she remembered when we went to a new duty station she told herself, "I'd better get acquainted and make some new friends fast because we won't be here long and we'll have to leave again soon."

Dave's next duty station was with 2nd Marines Regimental Headquarters, at Camp Lejeune, NC, for his second tour there.

All our kids were in high school by this time. On the first day of school, Becky came home looking down in the mouth, saying, "Mom, the high school is in the middle of a cornfield!" And all the kids talk like *grits*. I answered her, saying, "Well, no one throws prunes at you and you can understand them even if they do talk like grits. Do like the marines say, 'Suck it up!'" Becky married a Jacksonville young man a few years later, so she must have gotten used to grit talk.

The kids settled in and enjoyed their years at White Oak High School. They were all in band, and I didn't have to fight to get them in it. Since we had three there, I felt obligated to join band boosters. Becky was in several plays and graduated in 1978. She met her future husband at a dance at the high school.

Later on, Dave made Commander which meant he was to go to the senior course in Newport, Rhode Island for one year. We discussed and prayed about us moving there, too, since we were having a lot of problems with Carey's drinking. My husband didn't think I could handle it by myself, but we didn't want to move before Carey's senior and Laura's junior years. But Carey, Laura, and I went along with Dave, too. Becky was in college now, in Gardner Webb at Boiling Springs, North Carolina. We had mixed feelings about moving them but thought they'd adjust if we all stuck together. If we had it to do over again, I'd tough it out and stay in Jacksonville, North Carolina, so the kids wouldn't have to go through that experience they had in the high school in Rhode Island.

Little did we know that the high school they attended allowed alcohol and drugs in the classroom. Laura told us there were students in her class who were *stoned to the gills*, and it wasn't unusual to see some student hauled away in an ambulance, going to the emergency room from alcohol or drug overdose. The teachers never said or did anything about their drinking or using drugs, either. It seemed our kids would have *post-traumatic stress syndrome* just from trying to get a high school education!

After Dave finished the senior course, he received orders to the USS *America*, an aircraft carrier stationed in Norfolk, Virginia. We needed a house to live in and there wasn't much housing, so I flew down to Virginia Beach to look for a one. Becky met me on her spring break, so we searched for a house in the Kempsville area where we heard from other colleagues that it had the best school system. We found one being built, so we picked out carpet colors, wallpaper designs, etc. When we moved in, our neighbor told us the school system had been rezoned and Laura would go to a different school. What a bummer! But it was a brand-new school and she enjoyed it and graduated there the next spring.

Dave spent three years aboard the carrier, and when they were at sea, he preached many times on Sunday, going by helo to the other ships that were in their group. Dave had help with counseling on the ship, since there were three chaplains on board. There were two Protestants and one Catholic priest. When the pilots and aircraft were on board, there was a total of about 6,000 men. The carrier made many trips to the Caribbean and the Mediterranean, as well as going down the Suez Canal and into the Indian Ocean. Halfway through the seven-month cruise, several wives and myself met the ship when it landed in Perth, Australia. The Aussies are very kind, hospitable people, and I'd like to go back there for more than five days.

While Dave was on the America, we lost our son Carey. For a long while, I expected him to still come bounding through the front door and asking me, "What are we having for supper, Mom?" We still miss him greatly, even though it's been many years since he left us. But we have the promise that we'll be together again in heaven.

We remember the heartache which time has eased, but never erased.

Dave had back-to-back tours in Norfolk, so he was stationed there eight years. He retired on December 1, 1987 with twenty-two and a half years as a chaplain, four years as an enlisted man, and two years in the reserves.

Since Dave's military retirement, he pastored a Baptist church in Virginia Beach for three years. Then we felt called to serve as foreign missionaries in our fifties. We served five years in Morocco and three in Ukraine. When we told our daughter Laura that we felt the Lord calling us to the mission field, she said, "Well, it's better than joining the circus!"

We retired from the mission field, but now we're just shifting gears. When the Lord calls you to do full-time service, it doesn't end. We taught English as a second language to refugees and people that need to learn to read here in New Bern. Dave preaches when he gets an opportunity.

He learned that he has non-Hodgkin's lymphoma (caused by Agent Orange in Vietnam). He took chemo treatments for eight years, every six months. Now it's in remission but it's left him with severe neuropathy in his limbs.

For the military families, I'd say,
"No matter what the orders say…
Either off to war, air, or sailing on the sea,
Whether he or she's at sea or on land,
For heaven's sake, *stand by your man (or woman)!*"

45

VITAL STATS:
Name: David Garth Page
Born: Excelsior Springs, MO, Oct. 15, 1933
Education: SW Baptist College, AA, William Jewell College-BA, Southern Seminary-BD, Old Dominion University-MBA
Residence: New Bern, MC
Family: Wife, Gwyn; son, Carey (deceased); daughters, Becky and Laura; grandchildren, Sarah, Daniel, Beth, Amy, and Lillie; great-grand-children, James and David
Hobbies: Hunting, fishing, gardening

VITAL STATS:
Name: Gwyndolin Cloud Page
Born: Chicago, IL, Feb. 4, 1938
Education: SW Baptist College, William Jewell College, Baptist College of Charleston, ODU
Residence: New Bern, NC
Family: Husband, Dave; son, Carey (deceased); daughters: Becky and Laura; five grandchildren, two great-grandchildren
Hobbies: oil and acrylic painting, reading, writing

After Dave's conversion in 1955, he felt a need to put his feelings on paper. (Luckily, I just found these poems in a folder, along with the journal of his military activities.) So here are some poems he wrote that he hoped would one day be the lyrics to some country/ Western songs:

Written by David G. Page, 1955
While on the USS *Boxer*, USN

## My Friend

I'm a sailor for Jesus, for He is my friend.
Once I was lost, I was drowning in sin.
But I called to the lifeguard in heaven on high
And he hastened to answer my humble cry.
As I sail through this life, I have set my course
On the bright star of Jesus and I'll hold it with force.
Against waves of temptation and sin,
I'm sailing for Jesus, for He is my friend.

# Hillbilly Christian

I'm a hillbilly Christian as anyone can see.
I'll work for my Master till His face I see.
I'll lay up my treasures in that land beyond the sky.
I'm a hillbilly Christian until the day I die.

I was a sinner; my soul was lost.
Upon the sea of life, my ship was tossed.
But from that ship of sin, Christ lifted me.
Now I'm a hillbilly Christian and always shall be.

This is the story of one country kid
Who likes to tell of Jesus and the things that He did.
If you'll take Him as your savior,
from all sin you'll be free. Then you will love the Lord Jesus
And praise His name like me.

# Had He Not Died

Have you ever wondered how this world would be
If Christ had not died on Calvary's tree?
There would be no hope for a life after death.
Yes, we can thank Jesus for this precious gift.
He lay down His life that we might be saved.
To redeem our sins, so willingly He gave.

After doing all this for me, it would seem
That we should worship Him with the greatest esteem.
Usually you find the opposite effect,
As men treat His name with much disrespect.
They turn not to Him for the things of this life.

Since I have accepted the shelter of His fold,
My life has been a joy to behold.
For He is my strength as I labor each day.
And when my time is come, I shall go see
That glorious man that died for me.

The following poem is fictional and it was Dave's hope that it would someday be made into a ballad:

# A Ballad of Hope

I. Once I was married to a wonderful girl.
We had no treasures that count in this world.
But we have a mansion in our land in the sky,
And I know we will meet there in the sweet by and by.

II. Now my wife has left me in this world here below
To dwell with our landlord in His mansion of gold.
Someday I will follow to that wonderful land
When my life on this earth has completed God's plan.

III. Now we have a daughter whose age is just three,
And I teach her of Jesus, as she sits on my knee.
I pray she'll have the treasures in the next life
And dwell forever with me and my wife.

# *What Christmas Means to Me*

As we approach each Christmas season,
My heart is filled with joy, and this is the reason.
I've found a friend to walk with on the way.
He shows me the path, lest I wander away astray.

Not only a friend but a savior to us
Who have placed in Him our every trust.
Surely, you've heard of Him, of whom I write.
The one and only, the Lord Jesus Christ.

For us He was born, for us He has died.
For us He was raised up to His Father's side.
So now you can see why I'm so happy.
I pray because Christmas surely is our Lord's birthday.

Dave's 'crew' at home

Dave being high-lined from one ship to another

Cdr. David G. Page

After chaper service at Ben Marell housing complex

Dave's retirement ceremony Dec1, 1987

A Bible Study in the jungle

Chapel service in Chu Lai

LOOKING MORE LIKE AN UNCLE than a chaplain is Lt, Cmdr. David Page of Liberty who is pictured with more than a dozen orphan boys outside a church in the village of Tam Ky, Vietnam. The lads will be among the recipients of the clothing bundles which were sent from Liberty recently.

# Chaplains Help Refugees

By LCpl. Bill McClellan

CHU LAI — Everybody talks about the weather but it took the two chaplains of MAG-13 to do something about it.

"We knew we couldn't stop the monsoons from arriving," commented Navy Chaplain (Lieutenant Commander) David G. Page (Liberty, Mo.), "but we could help the refugee families prepare for the rain."

Before the two chaplains intervened, over five hundred Vietnamese families near Tam Ky had good reason to fear the rainy weather. The families, all of whom had fled Viet Cong controlled areas, were living in make-shift bamboo huts that could not withstand the heavy rain.

"When we heard about their situation we sent them a $150 donation from the chapel fund. A little later we were able to gather some lumber and tin so we sent that along, too," remarked Navy Chaplain (Lieutenant) Peter J. Cary (Milwaukee, Wis.).

Shortly after their initial donation, the two chaplains visited the refugee families.

"We were quite surprised at their ability to fashion homes so quickly out of the crude materials we had sent them," Lt. Cary said.

"We also realized that the material we had sent them merely scratched the surface of their needs," he added.

The chaplains then searched the Chu Lai Air Base for additional lumber and tin and accumulated sixteen truck loads of the material.

With the aid of a Vietnamese priest in Tam Ky, the chaplains were able to arrange delivery of the materials through ARVN soldiers.

"The architecture of the homes may leave something to be desired," chuckled LCdr. Page, "but they are waterproof now."

Due to the efforts of the MAG-13 chaplains, the gray monsoon skies will not look quite so bleak to the inhabitants.

## Catholic Orphanages Get Food

By LCpl. Sergio Ortiz

CHU LAI — A Protestant chaplain and a Catholic nun here have joined efforts to bring orphans a symbol of hope.

Navy Chaplain (Lieutenant Commander) David G. Page (Liberty, Mo.), of Mag-13, has transported over 600 cases of baby food to two Catholic orphanages in Van Co and Quang Ngai City.

Since Chaplain Page had never been in Quang Ngai City, he enlisted the aid of a Vietnamese nun to show th     y.

"We have be   iving aid to these two orphanages for nearly two years in the form of clothing or food whenever possible," LCdr. Page said.

The food was acquired through the chaplain at Mag-16 who received it from International Orphans Incorporated of Los Angeles.

The majority of children at the Van Co Orphanage, located near the Dickey Chappelle Memorial Dispensary, are left in    re of the nuns by families too     to support them.

Here are 600 boxes of baby food after it
was unloaded from the helicopter.

The Battalion Chaplain conducted Protestant services
in the field during the landing at Nea Peramos, Greece.
The city of Philllipi, which was visited by St. Paul in
the first century, isonly 30 miles from this site.

Preaching to Marine Battalion

Dave visiting with Greek Orthodox priest

Gwyn Page
1991—at appt. of IMB

1991—David G. Page
Appointment of IMB

# About the Author

G wyn and her husband married during their college years. Seminary followed, and not long after, she became a chaplain's wife. So she and her three children supported and followed when duty called her husband. Read about the experiences they encountered and the ways she dealt with new and changing circumstances.

CPSIA information can be obtained
at www.ICGtesting.com
Printed in the USA
JSHW021652090120
3416JS00004B/56